50 Savor the Seasons Recipes

By: Kelly Johnson

Table of Contents

- Spring Asparagus Risotto
- Summer Caprese Salad
- Autumn Pumpkin Soup
- Winter Beef Stew
- Grilled Peach Salad
- Zucchini Fritters
- Roasted Brussels Sprouts
- Strawberry Rhubarb Pie
- Spaghetti with Summer Tomatoes
- Butternut Squash Risotto
- Fall Apple Crisp
- Fresh Corn Chowder
- Grilled Salmon with Mango Salsa
- Roasted Beet Salad with Goat Cheese
- Carrot and Ginger Soup
- Roasted Sweet Potato Tacos
- Summer Grilled Veggie Skewers
- Spiced Pear Cake
- Pumpkin Pancakes
- Cucumber and Dill Salad
- Winter Squash and Kale Soup
- Pesto Pasta with Cherry Tomatoes
- Winter Citrus Salad
- Apple and Brie Grilled Cheese
- Garlic Herb Roasted Chicken
- Roasted Root Vegetables
- Summer Berry Tart
- Cabbage and Sausage Stew
- Lemon Blueberry Muffins
- Apple Cinnamon Oatmeal
- Winter Cranberry Sauce
- Grilled Chicken with Basil and Tomato
- Roasted Butternut Squash Salad
- Beetroot Hummus
- Spicy Pumpkin Curry

- Tomato Basil Soup
- Summer Vegetable Pasta
- Warm Kale Salad with Bacon
- Autumn Spiced Applesauce
- Lemon Herb Roasted Potatoes
- Grilled Chicken Caesar Salad
- Pear and Walnut Salad
- Honey Balsamic Roasted Carrots
- Spaghetti Squash Primavera
- Fresh Tomato Salsa
- Roasted Fig and Goat Cheese Salad
- Pumpkin Spice Bread
- Baked Apples with Cinnamon
- Strawberry Sorbet
- Grilled Apricot and Prosciutto Salad

Spring Asparagus Risotto

Ingredients:

- 1 lb asparagus, trimmed and cut into 2-inch pieces
- 2 tablespoons olive oil
- 1 small onion, finely chopped
- 1 1/2 cups Arborio rice
- 4 cups chicken or vegetable broth, kept warm
- 1/2 cup dry white wine
- 1/2 cup grated Parmesan cheese
- 2 tablespoons unsalted butter
- Salt and pepper to taste

Instructions:

1. In a large pan, heat olive oil over medium heat. Add onion and sauté until softened, about 5 minutes.
2. Add asparagus and cook for 2-3 minutes until tender but still vibrant green.
3. Stir in the Arborio rice and cook for 1-2 minutes to lightly toast the rice.
4. Pour in the white wine and cook until absorbed. Gradually add the warm broth, 1/2 cup at a time, stirring constantly until the liquid is absorbed before adding more.
5. Continue until the rice is creamy and cooked through, about 18-20 minutes.
6. Stir in Parmesan, butter, and season with salt and pepper. Serve warm.

Summer Caprese Salad

Ingredients:

- 4 ripe tomatoes, sliced
- 8 oz fresh mozzarella, sliced
- 1/4 cup fresh basil leaves
- 3 tablespoons balsamic vinegar
- 2 tablespoons olive oil
- Salt and pepper to taste

Instructions:

1. On a platter, alternate layers of tomato slices, mozzarella, and basil leaves.
2. Drizzle with olive oil and balsamic vinegar.
3. Season with salt and pepper, and serve chilled or at room temperature.

Autumn Pumpkin Soup

Ingredients:

- 1 medium pumpkin, peeled, seeded, and chopped
- 1 onion, chopped
- 2 cloves garlic, minced
- 4 cups vegetable or chicken broth
- 1/2 cup heavy cream
- 1 teaspoon ground cinnamon
- 1/2 teaspoon ground nutmeg
- Salt and pepper to taste
- Olive oil for roasting

Instructions:

1. Preheat the oven to 400°F (200°C). Toss the pumpkin chunks with olive oil and roast on a baking sheet for 25-30 minutes, or until tender.
2. In a large pot, sauté onion and garlic until softened. Add roasted pumpkin and broth, and bring to a simmer.
3. Use an immersion blender to blend the soup until smooth. Stir in heavy cream, cinnamon, nutmeg, salt, and pepper.
4. Simmer for an additional 5 minutes, then serve warm.

Winter Beef Stew

Ingredients:

- 2 lbs beef stew meat, cubed
- 2 tablespoons olive oil
- 1 onion, chopped
- 3 cloves garlic, minced
- 4 carrots, peeled and chopped
- 3 potatoes, peeled and cubed
- 2 cups beef broth
- 1 cup red wine
- 2 tablespoons tomato paste
- 1 teaspoon dried thyme
- Salt and pepper to taste

Instructions:

1. In a large pot, heat olive oil over medium-high heat. Brown the beef in batches, then set aside.
2. In the same pot, sauté onion and garlic until softened.
3. Add the beef back into the pot, along with carrots, potatoes, beef broth, red wine, tomato paste, thyme, salt, and pepper. Bring to a boil.
4. Reduce heat and simmer for 1.5-2 hours, or until the beef is tender. Serve hot.

Grilled Peach Salad

Ingredients:

- 4 ripe peaches, halved and pitted
- 4 cups mixed salad greens
- 1/4 cup goat cheese, crumbled
- 1/4 cup toasted pecans
- 2 tablespoons olive oil
- 1 tablespoon balsamic vinegar
- Salt and pepper to taste

Instructions:

1. Preheat the grill to medium heat. Grill the peach halves for 2-3 minutes on each side until grill marks appear.
2. In a large bowl, toss the salad greens with olive oil, balsamic vinegar, salt, and pepper.
3. Arrange the grilled peaches on top of the greens, and sprinkle with goat cheese and toasted pecans. Serve immediately.

Zucchini Fritters

Ingredients:

- 2 medium zucchinis, grated
- 1 small onion, grated
- 1/2 cup all-purpose flour
- 2 eggs
- 1/2 cup grated Parmesan cheese
- Salt and pepper to taste
- Olive oil for frying

Instructions:

1. Squeeze out excess moisture from the grated zucchini using a clean towel.
2. In a large bowl, combine zucchini, onion, flour, eggs, Parmesan, salt, and pepper.
3. Heat olive oil in a frying pan over medium heat. Drop spoonfuls of the zucchini mixture into the pan and flatten slightly.
4. Cook for 2-3 minutes on each side, until golden brown. Drain on paper towels and serve warm.

Roasted Brussels Sprouts

Ingredients:

- 1 lb Brussels sprouts, trimmed and halved
- 2 tablespoons olive oil
- 1 tablespoon balsamic vinegar
- Salt and pepper to taste

Instructions:

1. Preheat the oven to 400°F (200°C).
2. Toss the Brussels sprouts with olive oil, balsamic vinegar, salt, and pepper.
3. Roast for 20-25 minutes, shaking the pan halfway through, until the Brussels sprouts are crispy on the outside and tender on the inside.

Strawberry Rhubarb Pie

Ingredients:

- 1 1/2 cups chopped strawberries
- 1 1/2 cups chopped rhubarb
- 1 cup granulated sugar
- 2 tablespoons cornstarch
- 1 tablespoon lemon juice
- 1 tablespoon butter
- 1 package pie crusts (or homemade)

Instructions:

1. Preheat the oven to 425°F (220°C).
2. In a bowl, combine strawberries, rhubarb, sugar, cornstarch, and lemon juice. Stir until well mixed.
3. Roll out one pie crust and place it in a pie dish. Pour the strawberry-rhubarb filling into the crust.
4. Dot with butter and top with the second pie crust. Trim and crimp the edges, then cut slits in the top to allow steam to escape.
5. Bake for 45-50 minutes, or until the crust is golden brown. Let cool before serving.

Spaghetti with Summer Tomatoes

Ingredients:

- 1 lb spaghetti
- 2 cups cherry tomatoes, halved
- 3 tablespoons olive oil
- 3 cloves garlic, minced
- 1/4 cup fresh basil, chopped
- Salt and pepper to taste
- Grated Parmesan cheese, for serving

Instructions:

1. Cook spaghetti according to package instructions. Drain, reserving 1/2 cup pasta water.
2. In a large pan, heat olive oil over medium heat. Add garlic and cook for 1 minute until fragrant.
3. Add cherry tomatoes and cook for 5-7 minutes until softened.
4. Toss the cooked pasta into the tomato mixture, adding reserved pasta water as needed to loosen the sauce.
5. Stir in fresh basil, season with salt and pepper, and top with Parmesan cheese.

Butternut Squash Risotto

Ingredients:

- 1 small butternut squash, peeled, seeded, and cubed
- 2 tablespoons olive oil
- 1 small onion, chopped
- 1 1/2 cups Arborio rice
- 4 cups chicken or vegetable broth, kept warm
- 1/2 cup dry white wine
- 1/2 cup grated Parmesan cheese
- 2 tablespoons unsalted butter
- Salt and pepper to taste

Instructions:

1. Preheat the oven to 400°F (200°C). Toss cubed butternut squash with olive oil, salt, and pepper, then roast for 20-25 minutes until tender.
2. In a large pan, sauté onion in olive oil until softened. Add Arborio rice and cook for 1-2 minutes.
3. Pour in white wine and cook until absorbed. Gradually add warm broth, stirring constantly until absorbed before adding more.
4. Stir in roasted butternut squash, Parmesan, and butter. Season with salt and pepper to taste. Serve warm.

Fall Apple Crisp

Ingredients:

- 4 cups apples, peeled, cored, and sliced
- 1 tablespoon lemon juice
- 1/2 cup granulated sugar
- 1 teaspoon ground cinnamon
- 1/2 teaspoon ground nutmeg
- 1/4 teaspoon salt
- 1 cup old-fashioned oats
- 1/2 cup all-purpose flour
- 1/2 cup packed brown sugar
- 1/2 cup unsalted butter, melted

Instructions:

1. Preheat oven to 350°F (175°C). Grease a 9x9-inch baking dish.
2. In a bowl, toss the sliced apples with lemon juice, granulated sugar, cinnamon, nutmeg, and salt. Spread the mixture evenly in the prepared baking dish.
3. In another bowl, mix oats, flour, brown sugar, and melted butter until the mixture is crumbly.
4. Sprinkle the oat mixture over the apples.
5. Bake for 40-45 minutes, or until the top is golden and the apples are tender. Serve warm.

Fresh Corn Chowder

Ingredients:

- 4 cups fresh corn kernels (about 4 ears of corn)
- 1 tablespoon olive oil
- 1 onion, chopped
- 2 cloves garlic, minced
- 2 large potatoes, peeled and diced
- 4 cups vegetable broth
- 1 cup heavy cream
- 1 teaspoon thyme
- Salt and pepper to taste
- Fresh parsley, chopped for garnish

Instructions:

1. Heat olive oil in a large pot over medium heat. Add onion and garlic, cooking until softened, about 5 minutes.
2. Add potatoes and vegetable broth, bring to a boil, and simmer until potatoes are tender, about 15 minutes.
3. Stir in the corn kernels, thyme, salt, and pepper. Cook for an additional 5 minutes.
4. Reduce heat and stir in the heavy cream. Simmer for 5 more minutes.
5. Serve hot, garnished with fresh parsley.

Grilled Salmon with Mango Salsa

Ingredients:

- 4 salmon fillets
- 1 tablespoon olive oil
- Salt and pepper to taste
- 1 mango, peeled, pitted, and diced
- 1/4 cup red onion, finely chopped
- 1/4 cup cilantro, chopped
- 1 tablespoon lime juice

Instructions:

1. Preheat grill to medium-high heat. Brush the salmon fillets with olive oil and season with salt and pepper.
2. Grill the salmon for 4-5 minutes per side, or until cooked through.
3. In a bowl, combine mango, red onion, cilantro, and lime juice. Mix well.
4. Serve the grilled salmon with a generous spoonful of mango salsa on top.

Roasted Beet Salad with Goat Cheese

Ingredients:

- 4 medium beets, peeled and cut into cubes
- 1 tablespoon olive oil
- Salt and pepper to taste
- 4 cups mixed greens
- 1/4 cup goat cheese, crumbled
- 1/4 cup walnuts, toasted
- 2 tablespoons balsamic vinegar
- 1 tablespoon honey

Instructions:

1. Preheat oven to 400°F (200°C). Toss the beet cubes with olive oil, salt, and pepper. Spread them on a baking sheet.
2. Roast the beets for 25-30 minutes, stirring occasionally, until tender.
3. In a large bowl, toss the mixed greens with balsamic vinegar and honey. Add the roasted beets, goat cheese, and walnuts.
4. Serve immediately.

Carrot and Ginger Soup

Ingredients:

- 1 tablespoon olive oil
- 1 onion, chopped
- 3 cups carrots, peeled and chopped
- 2 cloves garlic, minced
- 1-inch piece fresh ginger, grated
- 4 cups vegetable broth
- Salt and pepper to taste
- Fresh parsley for garnish

Instructions:

1. Heat olive oil in a large pot over medium heat. Add onion, carrots, garlic, and ginger. Cook for 5 minutes, stirring occasionally.
2. Add vegetable broth, salt, and pepper. Bring to a boil, then reduce to a simmer for 15-20 minutes, until the carrots are tender.
3. Use an immersion blender to puree the soup until smooth.
4. Garnish with fresh parsley and serve.

Roasted Sweet Potato Tacos

Ingredients:

- 2 large sweet potatoes, peeled and cubed
- 2 tablespoons olive oil
- 1 teaspoon ground cumin
- 1 teaspoon chili powder
- Salt and pepper to taste
- 8 small corn tortillas
- 1/4 cup fresh cilantro, chopped
- 1/2 cup avocado, diced
- 1/4 cup sour cream (optional)
- 1 lime, cut into wedges

Instructions:

1. Preheat oven to 400°F (200°C). Toss sweet potato cubes with olive oil, cumin, chili powder, salt, and pepper. Spread on a baking sheet.
2. Roast for 25-30 minutes, or until tender and slightly caramelized.
3. Heat the tortillas in a dry skillet or on a griddle.
4. Assemble the tacos by filling each tortilla with roasted sweet potatoes, cilantro, avocado, and sour cream (if using).
5. Serve with lime wedges.

Summer Grilled Veggie Skewers

Ingredients:

- 1 zucchini, sliced
- 1 red bell pepper, cut into chunks
- 1 yellow bell pepper, cut into chunks
- 1 red onion, cut into chunks
- 8 oz mushrooms, whole
- 2 tablespoons olive oil
- 1 tablespoon balsamic vinegar
- Salt and pepper to taste
- 1 tablespoon fresh thyme

Instructions:

1. Preheat grill to medium-high heat.
2. Thread the vegetables onto skewers, alternating between the zucchini, peppers, onion, and mushrooms.
3. In a small bowl, whisk together olive oil, balsamic vinegar, salt, pepper, and thyme. Brush the vegetables with the marinade.
4. Grill the skewers for 8-10 minutes, turning occasionally, until the vegetables are tender and slightly charred.
5. Serve warm.

Spiced Pear Cake

Ingredients:

- 2 ripe pears, peeled and diced
- 1 1/2 cups all-purpose flour
- 1/2 teaspoon baking powder
- 1/2 teaspoon ground cinnamon
- 1/4 teaspoon ground nutmeg
- 1/4 teaspoon ground ginger
- 1/4 teaspoon salt
- 1/2 cup unsalted butter, softened
- 1/2 cup granulated sugar
- 2 large eggs
- 1 teaspoon vanilla extract
- 1/4 cup milk

Instructions:

1. Preheat oven to 350°F (175°C). Grease and flour an 8-inch round cake pan.
2. In a bowl, whisk together flour, baking powder, cinnamon, nutmeg, ginger, and salt.
3. In another bowl, cream together butter and sugar until light and fluffy. Add eggs one at a time, followed by vanilla extract.
4. Add the dry ingredients to the butter mixture, alternating with milk. Stir in diced pears.
5. Pour the batter into the prepared pan and bake for 35-40 minutes, or until a toothpick comes out clean.
6. Let the cake cool before serving.

Pumpkin Pancakes

Ingredients:

- 1 cup all-purpose flour
- 1 tablespoon sugar
- 2 teaspoons baking powder
- 1 teaspoon ground cinnamon
- 1/2 teaspoon ground nutmeg
- 1/2 teaspoon salt
- 1 cup milk
- 1/2 cup pumpkin puree
- 1 large egg
- 2 tablespoons melted butter
- 1 teaspoon vanilla extract

Instructions:

1. In a bowl, whisk together flour, sugar, baking powder, cinnamon, nutmeg, and salt.
2. In another bowl, mix milk, pumpkin puree, egg, melted butter, and vanilla extract.
3. Combine the wet and dry ingredients and stir until just combined (do not overmix).
4. Heat a griddle or non-stick skillet over medium heat. Lightly grease with butter.
5. Pour 1/4 cup of batter onto the skillet for each pancake. Cook until bubbles form on the surface, then flip and cook for another 1-2 minutes.
6. Serve warm with maple syrup.

Cucumber and Dill Salad

Ingredients:

- 2 large cucumbers, sliced
- 1/4 cup red onion, thinly sliced
- 1/4 cup fresh dill, chopped
- 2 tablespoons olive oil
- 1 tablespoon white wine vinegar
- Salt and pepper to taste

Instructions:

1. In a bowl, combine the cucumbers, red onion, and fresh dill.
2. Drizzle with olive oil and vinegar, and toss to coat.
3. Season with salt and pepper to taste.
4. Chill for 30 minutes before serving for the best flavor.

Winter Squash and Kale Soup

Ingredients:

- 1 medium butternut squash, peeled and cubed
- 1 tablespoon olive oil
- 1 onion, chopped
- 2 cloves garlic, minced
- 4 cups vegetable broth
- 2 cups kale, chopped
- 1 teaspoon ground cumin
- 1/2 teaspoon ground cinnamon
- Salt and pepper to taste
- 1/2 cup coconut milk (optional)

Instructions:

1. Preheat oven to 400°F (200°C). Toss the butternut squash cubes with olive oil, salt, and pepper. Roast on a baking sheet for 25-30 minutes, or until tender.
2. In a large pot, heat olive oil over medium heat. Add onion and garlic, cooking until softened, about 5 minutes.
3. Add the roasted squash, vegetable broth, cumin, and cinnamon. Bring to a boil and simmer for 10 minutes.
4. Stir in kale and cook for an additional 5 minutes until wilted.
5. For a smoother texture, blend the soup with an immersion blender or in batches in a regular blender.
6. Stir in coconut milk if desired and season with salt and pepper to taste. Serve hot.

Pesto Pasta with Cherry Tomatoes

Ingredients:

- 8 oz pasta (such as spaghetti or penne)
- 1 cup fresh basil leaves
- 1/4 cup pine nuts
- 1/4 cup grated Parmesan cheese
- 2 cloves garlic
- 1/4 cup olive oil
- 1 pint cherry tomatoes, halved
- Salt and pepper to taste

Instructions:

1. Cook the pasta according to package instructions. Drain, reserving 1/2 cup pasta water.
2. In a food processor, combine basil, pine nuts, Parmesan, garlic, and olive oil. Blend until smooth. Add salt and pepper to taste.
3. In a large pan, heat the pesto over medium heat. Toss the cooked pasta into the pan, adding a little reserved pasta water if needed to thin the sauce.
4. Stir in cherry tomatoes and cook for 2-3 minutes, just until they soften.
5. Serve with extra Parmesan if desired.

Winter Citrus Salad

Ingredients:

- 2 grapefruits, peeled and segmented
- 2 oranges, peeled and segmented
- 1/2 small red onion, thinly sliced
- 1/4 cup pomegranate seeds
- 1/4 cup fresh mint leaves
- 2 tablespoons olive oil
- 1 tablespoon honey
- Salt and pepper to taste

Instructions:

1. In a large bowl, combine grapefruit, orange segments, red onion, pomegranate seeds, and mint leaves.
2. In a small bowl, whisk together olive oil, honey, salt, and pepper. Drizzle over the salad and toss gently.
3. Serve immediately or chill for 10 minutes before serving.

Apple and Brie Grilled Cheese

Ingredients:

- 4 slices sourdough bread
- 2 tablespoons unsalted butter, softened
- 4 oz Brie cheese, sliced
- 1 apple, thinly sliced
- 1 tablespoon honey
- Salt and pepper to taste

Instructions:

1. Butter one side of each slice of bread. On the unbuttered side, layer the Brie cheese, apple slices, and drizzle with honey.
2. Close the sandwich and cook in a skillet over medium heat until golden brown and the cheese is melted, about 3-4 minutes per side.
3. Season with salt and pepper, slice, and serve warm.

Garlic Herb Roasted Chicken

Ingredients:

- 1 whole chicken (about 4 lbs)
- 4 cloves garlic, minced
- 1 tablespoon fresh thyme, chopped
- 1 tablespoon fresh rosemary, chopped
- 2 tablespoons olive oil
- 1 lemon, halved
- Salt and pepper to taste

Instructions:

1. Preheat oven to 425°F (220°C).
2. Pat the chicken dry and place it in a roasting pan.
3. In a small bowl, combine garlic, thyme, rosemary, olive oil, salt, and pepper. Rub this mixture all over the chicken.
4. Stuff the chicken cavity with the lemon halves.
5. Roast the chicken for 1 hour and 15 minutes, or until the internal temperature reaches 165°F (75°C). Let it rest for 10 minutes before carving.

Roasted Root Vegetables

Ingredients:

- 2 medium carrots, peeled and chopped
- 2 parsnips, peeled and chopped
- 1 sweet potato, peeled and chopped
- 1 tablespoon olive oil
- 1 teaspoon dried thyme
- Salt and pepper to taste

Instructions:

1. Preheat oven to 400°F (200°C). Line a baking sheet with parchment paper.
2. Toss the root vegetables with olive oil, thyme, salt, and pepper.
3. Spread the vegetables in a single layer on the baking sheet.
4. Roast for 30-40 minutes, stirring halfway through, until tender and caramelized.

Summer Berry Tart

Ingredients:

- 1 pre-made tart crust (or homemade)
- 1/2 cup heavy cream
- 8 oz cream cheese, softened
- 1/4 cup powdered sugar
- 1 teaspoon vanilla extract
- 2 cups mixed berries (strawberries, blueberries, raspberries, etc.)

Instructions:

1. Preheat oven to 350°F (175°C) and bake the tart crust according to package instructions or your recipe.
2. In a bowl, beat together cream cheese, powdered sugar, and vanilla extract until smooth.
3. In a separate bowl, whip the heavy cream until stiff peaks form. Fold the whipped cream into the cream cheese mixture.
4. Spread the cream mixture evenly into the cooled tart crust.
5. Top with fresh berries and serve chilled.

Cabbage and Sausage Stew

Ingredients:

- 1 tablespoon olive oil
- 1 lb sausage (such as Italian or kielbasa), sliced
- 1 onion, chopped
- 1/2 head of cabbage, shredded
- 2 carrots, peeled and sliced
- 4 cups chicken broth
- 1 teaspoon dried thyme
- Salt and pepper to taste

Instructions:

1. Heat olive oil in a large pot over medium heat. Add sausage slices and cook until browned, about 5 minutes.
2. Add onion, carrots, and cabbage. Cook for an additional 5 minutes.
3. Add chicken broth, thyme, salt, and pepper. Bring to a boil, then reduce to a simmer for 20-25 minutes until vegetables are tender.
4. Serve hot.

Lemon Blueberry Muffins

Ingredients:

- 2 cups all-purpose flour
- 3/4 cup granulated sugar
- 1 tablespoon baking powder
- 1/2 teaspoon salt
- 1/2 teaspoon baking soda
- 1/2 cup milk
- 1/2 cup unsalted butter, melted
- 2 large eggs
- 1 teaspoon vanilla extract
- Zest of 1 lemon
- 1 1/2 cups fresh blueberries

Instructions:

1. Preheat oven to 350°F (175°C). Line a muffin tin with paper liners.
2. In a large bowl, whisk together flour, sugar, baking powder, salt, and baking soda.
3. In another bowl, whisk together milk, melted butter, eggs, vanilla, and lemon zest.
4. Pour the wet ingredients into the dry ingredients and stir until just combined.
5. Gently fold in blueberries.
6. Spoon the batter into the muffin tin and bake for 18-22 minutes, or until a toothpick comes out clean.
7. Let cool before serving.

Apple Cinnamon Oatmeal

Ingredients:

- 1 apple, peeled and chopped
- 1 tablespoon butter
- 1 teaspoon cinnamon
- 1 cup rolled oats
- 2 cups milk (or water)
- 1 tablespoon honey (optional)
- A pinch of salt

Instructions:

1. In a small pan, melt butter over medium heat. Add apple and cinnamon, cooking until the apples soften, about 5 minutes.
2. In a separate pot, combine oats, milk, and salt. Bring to a boil, then reduce to a simmer, cooking until the oats are tender and the liquid is absorbed, about 5-7 minutes.
3. Stir in the cooked apples and honey, if using.
4. Serve warm.

Winter Cranberry Sauce

Ingredients:

- 12 oz fresh cranberries
- 1 cup orange juice
- 1/2 cup granulated sugar
- 1/4 cup honey
- Zest of 1 orange
- 1/2 teaspoon cinnamon

Instructions:

1. In a saucepan, combine cranberries, orange juice, sugar, honey, orange zest, and cinnamon.
2. Bring to a boil, then reduce heat and simmer for 10-15 minutes, or until the cranberries burst and the sauce thickens.
3. Let the sauce cool before serving.

Grilled Chicken with Basil and Tomato

Ingredients:

- 2 boneless, skinless chicken breasts
- 1 tablespoon olive oil
- 2 garlic cloves, minced
- Salt and pepper to taste
- 2 cups cherry tomatoes, halved
- 1/4 cup fresh basil, chopped
- 1 tablespoon balsamic vinegar

Instructions:

1. Preheat the grill to medium-high heat. Rub the chicken breasts with olive oil, garlic, salt, and pepper.
2. Grill the chicken for 6-7 minutes per side, or until fully cooked (internal temperature should reach 165°F).
3. While the chicken is grilling, combine the halved cherry tomatoes, basil, and balsamic vinegar in a bowl.
4. Once the chicken is cooked, top with the tomato-basil mixture and serve immediately.

Roasted Butternut Squash Salad

Ingredients:

- 1 small butternut squash, peeled, seeded, and cubed
- 1 tablespoon olive oil
- Salt and pepper to taste
- 2 cups mixed greens (arugula, spinach, etc.)
- 1/4 cup pomegranate seeds
- 1/4 cup crumbled feta cheese
- 1/4 cup walnuts, toasted
- 2 tablespoons balsamic glaze

Instructions:

1. Preheat oven to 400°F (200°C). Toss the cubed butternut squash with olive oil, salt, and pepper, then spread it on a baking sheet in a single layer.
2. Roast for 25-30 minutes, flipping halfway through, until tender and lightly browned.
3. In a large bowl, toss the roasted butternut squash with the mixed greens, pomegranate seeds, feta, and walnuts.
4. Drizzle with balsamic glaze before serving.

Beetroot Hummus

Ingredients:

- 1 can (15 oz) chickpeas, drained and rinsed
- 1 medium beetroot, cooked and peeled
- 2 tablespoons tahini
- 2 tablespoons olive oil
- 1 garlic clove
- 1 tablespoon lemon juice
- Salt and pepper to taste
- Water, as needed to adjust consistency

Instructions:

1. In a food processor, combine chickpeas, beetroot, tahini, olive oil, garlic, and lemon juice.
2. Blend until smooth, adding water a tablespoon at a time until desired consistency is reached.
3. Season with salt and pepper, then serve with pita or vegetable sticks.

Spicy Pumpkin Curry

Ingredients:

- 1 tablespoon vegetable oil
- 1 onion, chopped
- 2 cloves garlic, minced
- 1 tablespoon ginger, grated
- 1 can (15 oz) pumpkin puree
- 1 can (14 oz) coconut milk
- 1 tablespoon curry powder
- 1/2 teaspoon cayenne pepper (optional, for heat)
- Salt to taste
- Fresh cilantro, for garnish

Instructions:

1. Heat the vegetable oil in a large pot over medium heat. Add onion and cook until softened, about 5 minutes.
2. Add garlic and ginger and cook for another minute.
3. Stir in pumpkin puree, coconut milk, curry powder, cayenne pepper (if using), and salt. Bring to a simmer and cook for 15-20 minutes.
4. Garnish with fresh cilantro and serve with rice or naan.

Tomato Basil Soup

Ingredients:

- 1 tablespoon olive oil
- 1 onion, chopped
- 2 cloves garlic, minced
- 1 can (28 oz) crushed tomatoes
- 2 cups vegetable broth
- 1/2 cup heavy cream
- 1/4 cup fresh basil, chopped
- Salt and pepper to taste

Instructions:

1. Heat olive oil in a large pot over medium heat. Add onion and cook until softened, about 5 minutes.
2. Add garlic and cook for another minute.
3. Stir in crushed tomatoes and vegetable broth. Bring to a simmer and cook for 15 minutes.
4. Use an immersion blender or regular blender to puree the soup until smooth.
5. Stir in heavy cream, basil, salt, and pepper. Serve hot.

Summer Vegetable Pasta

Ingredients:

- 8 oz pasta (spaghetti or penne)
- 1 tablespoon olive oil
- 1 zucchini, chopped
- 1 yellow squash, chopped
- 1 bell pepper, chopped
- 1 cup cherry tomatoes, halved
- 2 garlic cloves, minced
- Salt and pepper to taste
- Fresh basil, for garnish
- Grated Parmesan cheese, for serving

Instructions:

1. Cook pasta according to package instructions. Drain, reserving 1/2 cup of pasta water.
2. Heat olive oil in a large pan over medium heat. Add zucchini, squash, bell pepper, and garlic. Cook for 5-7 minutes, until softened.
3. Add cherry tomatoes and cook for another 2 minutes until they soften.
4. Toss in the cooked pasta, adding reserved pasta water as needed. Season with salt and pepper.
5. Serve with fresh basil and grated Parmesan.

Warm Kale Salad with Bacon

Ingredients:

- 4 cups kale, chopped
- 4 slices bacon
- 1 tablespoon olive oil
- 1 tablespoon apple cider vinegar
- 1 teaspoon Dijon mustard
- Salt and pepper to taste

Instructions:

1. Cook bacon in a skillet over medium heat until crispy. Remove from the pan and crumble.
2. In the same pan, add olive oil and warm the kale until wilted, about 3-4 minutes.
3. In a small bowl, whisk together apple cider vinegar, Dijon mustard, salt, and pepper.
4. Toss the warm kale with the dressing, crumbled bacon, and serve immediately.

Autumn Spiced Applesauce

Ingredients:

- 6 apples, peeled, cored, and chopped
- 1/4 cup water
- 1/4 cup brown sugar
- 1 teaspoon ground cinnamon
- 1/4 teaspoon ground nutmeg
- 1/4 teaspoon ground cloves

Instructions:

1. In a large pot, combine apples, water, brown sugar, cinnamon, nutmeg, and cloves.
2. Cover and cook over medium heat for 25-30 minutes, stirring occasionally, until the apples are soft.
3. Mash with a potato masher for a chunky applesauce or blend for a smoother texture.
4. Serve warm or chilled.

Lemon Herb Roasted Potatoes

Ingredients:

- 1 1/2 lbs baby potatoes, halved
- 2 tablespoons olive oil
- 1 teaspoon fresh rosemary, chopped
- 1 teaspoon fresh thyme, chopped
- 1 lemon, zest and juice
- Salt and pepper to taste

Instructions:

1. Preheat oven to 400°F (200°C). Toss the potatoes with olive oil, rosemary, thyme, lemon zest, lemon juice, salt, and pepper.
2. Spread the potatoes in a single layer on a baking sheet.
3. Roast for 25-30 minutes, flipping halfway through, until golden and crispy.
4. Serve warm.

Grilled Chicken Caesar Salad

Ingredients:

- 2 boneless, skinless chicken breasts
- 1 tablespoon olive oil
- Salt and pepper to taste
- 4 cups romaine lettuce, chopped
- 1/4 cup grated Parmesan cheese
- Croutons, for topping
- Caesar dressing, to taste

Instructions:

1. Preheat the grill to medium-high heat. Rub the chicken breasts with olive oil, salt, and pepper.
2. Grill the chicken for 6-7 minutes per side, or until fully cooked (internal temperature should reach 165°F).
3. Slice the chicken into strips and toss with chopped romaine lettuce, Parmesan, and croutons.
4. Drizzle with Caesar dressing and serve immediately.

Pear and Walnut Salad

Ingredients:

- 4 cups mixed greens (arugula, spinach, etc.)
- 2 pears, sliced
- 1/2 cup walnuts, toasted
- 1/4 cup crumbled blue cheese or goat cheese
- 1/4 cup balsamic vinaigrette

Instructions:

1. In a large bowl, toss the mixed greens, pear slices, toasted walnuts, and cheese.
2. Drizzle with balsamic vinaigrette and toss gently to combine.
3. Serve immediately.

Honey Balsamic Roasted Carrots

Ingredients:

- 1 lb carrots, peeled and cut into sticks
- 1 tablespoon olive oil
- 1 tablespoon honey
- 1 tablespoon balsamic vinegar
- Salt and pepper to taste
- Fresh thyme (optional)

Instructions:

1. Preheat the oven to 400°F (200°C).
2. In a large bowl, toss the carrots with olive oil, honey, balsamic vinegar, salt, and pepper.
3. Spread the carrots in a single layer on a baking sheet.
4. Roast for 25-30 minutes, stirring halfway through, until tender and caramelized.
5. Garnish with fresh thyme and serve warm.

Spaghetti Squash Primavera

Ingredients:

- 1 medium spaghetti squash
- 1 tablespoon olive oil
- 1 zucchini, sliced
- 1 bell pepper, chopped
- 1/2 cup cherry tomatoes, halved
- 2 garlic cloves, minced
- 1/4 cup fresh basil, chopped
- Salt and pepper to taste
- Grated Parmesan cheese (optional)

Instructions:

1. Preheat the oven to 400°F (200°C). Slice the spaghetti squash in half lengthwise and scoop out the seeds.
2. Drizzle with olive oil, salt, and pepper. Place cut-side down on a baking sheet and roast for 35-40 minutes, or until tender.
3. While the squash is roasting, heat olive oil in a pan over medium heat. Add zucchini, bell pepper, and garlic, cooking for 5-7 minutes.
4. Once the squash is cooked, scrape the flesh with a fork to create spaghetti-like strands.
5. Toss the spaghetti squash strands with the sautéed vegetables, cherry tomatoes, basil, and grated Parmesan.
6. Serve warm.

Fresh Tomato Salsa

Ingredients:

- 4 ripe tomatoes, diced
- 1/2 onion, finely chopped
- 1 jalapeño, seeded and finely chopped (optional)
- 2 tablespoons fresh cilantro, chopped
- 1 tablespoon lime juice
- Salt to taste

Instructions:

1. In a bowl, combine tomatoes, onion, jalapeño, cilantro, and lime juice.
2. Season with salt and toss to combine.
3. Serve with tortilla chips, tacos, or as a topping for grilled meats.

Roasted Fig and Goat Cheese Salad

Ingredients:

- 6 figs, halved
- 2 tablespoons olive oil
- 1 tablespoon honey
- 4 cups mixed greens (arugula, spinach, etc.)
- 1/4 cup goat cheese, crumbled
- 1/4 cup walnuts, toasted
- Balsamic vinaigrette for drizzling

Instructions:

1. Preheat the oven to 375°F (190°C). Arrange fig halves on a baking sheet, drizzle with olive oil and honey.
2. Roast for 15-20 minutes, until soft and caramelized.
3. Toss the mixed greens with goat cheese, walnuts, and roasted figs.
4. Drizzle with balsamic vinaigrette and serve immediately.

Pumpkin Spice Bread

Ingredients:

- 1 3/4 cups all-purpose flour
- 1 teaspoon baking soda
- 1/2 teaspoon baking powder
- 1 teaspoon ground cinnamon
- 1/2 teaspoon ground nutmeg
- 1/4 teaspoon ground cloves
- 1/4 teaspoon salt
- 1 cup pumpkin puree
- 1/2 cup vegetable oil
- 3/4 cup granulated sugar
- 1/4 cup brown sugar
- 2 eggs
- 1 teaspoon vanilla extract
- 1/2 cup chopped walnuts (optional)

Instructions:

1. Preheat the oven to 350°F (175°C) and grease a 9x5-inch loaf pan.
2. In a bowl, whisk together flour, baking soda, baking powder, cinnamon, nutmeg, cloves, and salt.
3. In a separate bowl, whisk together pumpkin puree, vegetable oil, granulated sugar, brown sugar, eggs, and vanilla.
4. Gradually add the dry ingredients to the wet ingredients and mix until just combined.
5. Fold in walnuts if using.
6. Pour the batter into the prepared loaf pan and bake for 60-65 minutes, or until a toothpick inserted into the center comes out clean.
7. Cool before slicing and serving.

Baked Apples with Cinnamon

Ingredients:

- 4 apples, cored
- 1/4 cup brown sugar
- 1 teaspoon ground cinnamon
- 1 tablespoon butter, cubed
- 1/4 cup chopped walnuts or raisins (optional)

Instructions:

1. Preheat the oven to 350°F (175°C).
2. Place the cored apples in a baking dish.
3. In a small bowl, mix brown sugar, cinnamon, and walnuts or raisins (if using).
4. Stuff the apples with the sugar mixture and top with a cube of butter.
5. Cover with foil and bake for 30-40 minutes, until the apples are tender.
6. Serve warm with whipped cream or vanilla ice cream.

Strawberry Sorbet

Ingredients:

- 3 cups fresh strawberries, hulled
- 3/4 cup granulated sugar
- 1 tablespoon lemon juice
- 1/2 cup water

Instructions:

1. In a blender or food processor, combine strawberries, sugar, lemon juice, and water.
2. Blend until smooth, then transfer to a bowl and chill in the freezer for 2-3 hours.
3. Stir the sorbet every 30 minutes to break up any ice crystals. After 2-3 hours, it should have a soft, scoopable consistency.
4. Serve immediately or store in an airtight container.

Grilled Apricot and Prosciutto Salad

Ingredients:

- 4 apricots, halved and pitted
- 4 slices prosciutto
- 4 cups mixed greens (arugula, spinach, etc.)
- 1/4 cup crumbled goat cheese
- 2 tablespoons balsamic glaze
- 1 tablespoon olive oil
- Salt and pepper to taste

Instructions:

1. Preheat the grill or grill pan to medium heat.
2. Drizzle apricot halves with olive oil and season with salt and pepper.
3. Grill the apricots for 3-4 minutes on each side, until grill marks appear and they are slightly softened.
4. On a platter, arrange the mixed greens, grilled apricots, prosciutto, and goat cheese.
5. Drizzle with balsamic glaze and serve immediately.

www.ingramcontent.com/pod-product-compliance
Lightning Source LLC
LaVergne TN
LVHW061956070526
838199LV00060B/4154